Asian Elephant

Louise and Richard Spilsbury

Heinemann
LIBRARY

www.heinemann.co.uk/library
Visit our website to find out more information about Heinemann Library books.

To order:
☎ Phone 44 (0) 1865 888066
📄 Send a fax to 44 (0) 1865 314091
💻 Visit the Heinemann Bookshop at www.heinemann.co.uk/library to browse our catalogue and order online.

First published in Great Britain by Heinemann Library, Halley Court, Jordan Hill, Oxford OX2 8EJ, part of Harcourt Education.
Heinemann is a registered trademark of Harcourt Education Ltd.

Editorial: Kate Bellamy, Diyan Leake, Cassie Mayer, and Katie Shepherd
Design: Michelle Lisseter and Ron Kamen
Illustrations: Bridge Creative Services
Cartographer: Vickie Taylor at International Mapping
Picture research: Hannah Taylor and Fiona Orbell
Production: Duncan Gilbert

Origination: Chroma Graphics (Overseas) Pte. Ltd
Printed and bound in China by South China Printing Co. Ltd

The paper used to print this book comes from sustainable resources.

10 digit ISBN 0 431 11421 8 (hardback)
13 digit ISBN 978 0 431 11421 7
10 09 08 07 06
10 9 8 7 6 5 4 3 2 1

10 digit ISBN 0 431 11429 3 (paperback)
13 digit ISBN 978 0 431 11429 3
11 10 09 08 07
10 9 8 7 6 5 4 3 2 1

British Library Cataloguing in Publication Data
Spilsbury, Louise and Richard
Save the Asian elephant. – (Save our animals!)
599.6' 76
A full catalogue record for this book is available from the British Library.

Acknowledgements
The publishers would like to thank the following for permission to reproduce photographs: Ardea pp. **4** top (Y A Betrand), **5** top left, **13**, **26–27**, **29** (J Rajput), **22**; Steve Bloom p. **28**; Corbis p. **25** (M Harvey); Digital Vision p. **5** middle; Ecoscene p. **10** (W Lawler); FLPA p. **15** (J Zimmerman); Naturepl.com p. **4** bottom left (M Carwardine); NHPA pp. **12** (N Garbutt), **23** (A & S Toon); Oxford Scientific pp. **4** middle, **5** top right, **6**, **7** (S Camazine), **9** (M Brooke), **11** (Animals Animals), **14** (D Murrell), **16** (M Sewell), **18** (A Desai), **21**, **24**; Panos Pictures p. **19** (A Vitale); Still Pictures pp. **5** bottom; **17** (J Kaplan).

Cover photograph of Asian elephant, reproduced with permission of NHPA/Andy Rouse.

The publishers would like to thank Sarala Khaling at WWF in Nepal for her assistance in the preparation of this book.

Every effort has been made to contact copyright holders of any material reproduced in this book. Any omissions will be rectified in subsequent printings if notice is given to the publishers.

Contents

Some words are shown in bold, **like this**. You can find out what they mean by looking in the Glossary.

Animals in trouble

There are many different kinds, or **species**, of animal. Some species are in danger of becoming **extinct**. This means that all the animals from that species might die.

All the animals shown here are in danger of becoming extinct. These species need to be saved. The Asian elephant is one of them.

The Asian elephant

Elephants have a huge grey body and big ears. They use their long trunk for smelling, touching, and holding things.

An adult Asian elephant weighs the same as 50 men.

*Some **male** Asian elephants have two long teeth called **tusks**.*

There are African elephants and Asian elephants. The Asian elephant has a shorter trunk and smaller ears than the African elephant.

Where can you find Asian elephants?

Asian elephants live in thirteen of the countries on the **continent** of **Asia**. Over half of all Asian elephants live in India.

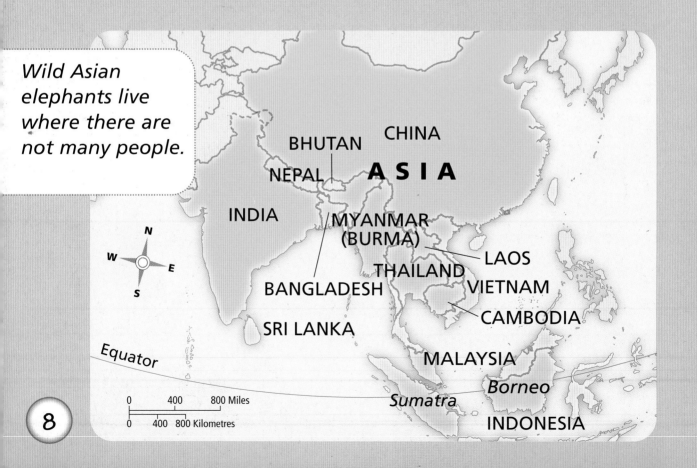

Wild Asian elephants live where there are not many people.

BHUTAN

CHINA

NEPAL

A S I A

INDIA

MYANMAR (BURMA)

LAOS

THAILAND

VIETNAM

BANGLADESH

CAMBODIA

SRI LANKA

MALAYSIA

Equator

Borneo

0   400   800 Miles

Sumatra

0   400   800 Kilometres

INDONESIA

Asian elephants drink water from pools or rivers.

Asian elephants live in forests where there are patches of long grass between the trees. It is usually hot and dry there. This is the Asian elephant's **habitat**.

What do Asian elephants eat?

Elephants are **herbivores**, which means they only eat plants. Elephants eat grass, leaves, and **roots**. They also eat **bark** and fruit from trees.

Elephants spend most of the day eating.

Every day, Asian elephants eat the same weight of food as 600 loaves of bread!

Elephants sometimes use their trunk to reach leaves at the top of trees. Then they put the leaves into their mouth with their trunk.

Young Asian elephants

A baby elephant is called a calf. An elephant calf can stand up soon after it is born. After two or three days, it can follow its mother around.

Elephants are **mammals**, so the babies drink their mother's milk.

Adult elephants protect the calves from attack.

Asian elephants live in a group called a herd. The babies grow up and play together. The adults in the herd look after the young elephants.

Working elephants

It is against the law to catch wild elephants but some people still do. They make the elephants carry big logs. The elephants sometimes die from working too hard.

Elephants can carry logs where trucks cannot go.

Sometimes, people make wild elephants work in a circus. Some get ill and die. Others die because they do not get the right food, or enough room to exercise.

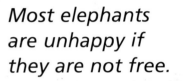

Most elephants are unhappy if they are not free.

Hunting Asian elephants

People used to kill **male** Asian elephants to get their **tusks**. Tusks are made of **ivory**. People carved the ivory or made piano keys from it.

Some ivory is used to make items like these.

Some people hunt elephants for their skin and meat. The skin can be made into bags and boots. Sometimes people use it to make **traditional** medicines.

Dangers to the Asian elephant's world

Asian elephants are losing their **habitat**. People are cutting down the forests where the elephants live. They use the wood to build towns there.

When forests are cut down, elephants have less space and less food.

Asian elephants may eat farmers' **crops** and damage people's homes. People sometimes kill the elephants to stop them.

Families go hungry if elephants damage their food plants.

How many Asian elephants are there?

Around 100 years ago there were more than 100,000 Asian elephants living in the wild. Today, there are only about 35,000 wild Asian elephants.

This graph shows how many Asian elephants there are.

🐘 = 20,000

The number of
Asian elephants
in the wild is still
going down.

Adult Asian elephants are not in danger
from other animals. They are too big
and strong. They are in danger of
becoming **extinct** because people do
not look after them or their **habitat**.

How are Asian elephants being saved?

Some countries have areas of land where elephants are safe and their **habitat** is looked after. These areas are called **national parks**.

National parks are big because the elephants and other animals there need lots of space.

These wardens stop poachers from killing elephants.

Poachers kill elephants for the ivory from their **tusks**. **Wardens** carry weapons because it is their job to stop the poachers.

Who is helping Asian elephants?

Groups of people are working to save the elephants. They raise money to pay for safe areas for them. They help to train vets who can help if they are sick.

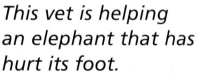

This vet is helping an elephant that has hurt its foot.

WWF is a group that works to protect elephant **habitats.** It plants new trees. It also helps people understand why elephants need to be saved.

People need to learn how to protect elephants.

How can you help?

It is important to know that Asian elephants are in danger. Then you can learn how to help save them. Read, watch, and find out all you can about Asian elephants.

Here are some things you can do
to help.

- Join a group that raises money for Asian elephants, such as **WWF**.
- Never buy **ivory** souvenirs.

The future for Asian elephants

There are very few wild elephants left in **Asia**. In the future there may be none at all. There will only be working elephants, or elephants in zoos.

These painted elephants are ready for an elephant festival.

Let's hope that more Asian elephants like these will be safe in the future.

People should stop buying and selling **ivory**. We should protect elephants in **national parks**. Then the number of Asian elephants will grow again.

Asian elephant facts

- Asian elephants can live for about 60 years in the wild.
- An elephant's trunk can lift heavy logs but it can also pick up things as small as a coin.
- Elephants are good swimmers. They can swim for several hours without a break.
- An elephant drinks by sucking the water up into its trunk and blowing it into its mouth.

More books to read

Asian Elephants, Matt Turner (Heinemann Library, 2004)

Hansa: The True Story of an Asian Elephant Baby, Clare Hodgson Meeker (Sasquatch Books, 2002)

Life in a Herd: Elephants, Richard and Louise Spilsbury (Heinemann, 2004)

Websites

To find out more about **WWF,** visit their website:

www.wwf.org

Glossary

Asia   the largest continent in the world

bark   hard layer that covers a tree trunk

continent   a large area of land divided into different countries

crop   plant grown for food, such as bananas

extinct   when all the animals in a species die out and the species no longer exists

habitat   place where plants and animals grow and live

herbivore   animal that only eats plants

ivory   hard, white material that tusks are made of

male   animal that can become a father when it grows up. Men and boys are male people.

mammal   animal that feeds its babies with the mother's milk and has some hair on its body

national park   area of land where animals are protected and their habitat is looked after

poacher   someone who hunts animals when it is against the law to do so

root   the part of a plant that grows underground

species   group of animals that look similar and can have babies together

traditional   something that has been done the same way for many years

tusk   long pointed front tooth of an elephant

warden   person who guards national parks

WWF   charity that used to be known as the World Wildlife Fund

Index